Funeral Services

of the Christian
Churches in England

Including additional hymn section

THE CANTERBURY PRESS NORWICH

The Canterbury Press Norwich
St Mary's Works, St Mary's Plain, Norwich, Norfolk NR3 3BH

The Canterbury Press Norwich is a publishing imprint of Hymns Ancient and
Modern Limited

ISBN 1 85311 095 7

Second Impression 1987
Third Impression 1988
Fourth Impression 1990
Fifth Impression, including new Roman Catholic Funeral Rite 1992
Sixth Impression 1993
New Edition 1994, including additional hymn section

Typeset by CCC, printed and bound in Great Britain by William Clowes Limited,
Beccles and London

CONTENTS

CHURCHES REPRESENTED ON THE CHURCHES' GROUP ON FUNERAL SERVICES AT CEMETERIES AND CREMATORIA

The Baptist Union of Great Britain and Ireland
The Church in Wales
The Church of England
The Methodist Church
The Roman Catholic Church
The United Reformed Church

in consultation with
The Free Church Council of Wales

PREFACE

In the compilation of this book the primary aim has been to make it as helpful as possible to those who are suffering under the burden and stress of grief. If this has been achieved it will incidentally assist those who are responsible for the ordering of services at cemeteries and crematoria.

Many who are faced with the loss of someone they have loved may not be able to bring to their situation the hope and strength of a well-tested and familiar religious faith. For them these services may afford perhaps not only comfort and support but also an opportunity for reflection and fresh spiritual understanding.

Whilst first and foremost the preparation of the book has been an exercise in ecumenical co-operation it has at the same time involved consultation with a number of those organisations which share responsibility with the Churches for the arrangement of funeral services. The Churches' Group on Funeral Services (the Churches' representative body on whose initiative the book has been published) wishes to record its warm appreciation of the wisdom, skill and dedication of all who in any capacity have taken part in this work.

Among them, special gratitude is due to the publishers, the Canterbury Press Norwich.

Funeral Service

prepared by the Joint Liturgical Group

INTRODUCTORY SENTENCES

One or more of the following sentences is said.

I am the resurrection and the life, says the Lord; he who believes in me, though he die, yet shall he live, and whoever lives and believes in me shall never die. *John 11.25-26*

The eternal God is your dwelling place, and underneath are the everlasting arms. *Deuteronomy 33.27*

I will never fail you nor forsake you, says the Lord. *Joshua 1.5*

Cast your burden on the Lord, and he will sustain you. *Psalm 55.22*

God is our refuge and strength, a very present help in trouble. *Psalm 46.1*

In his favour is life; weeping may endure for a night, but joy comes with the morning. *Psalm 30.5*

Blessed are those who mourn, for they shall be comforted. *Matthew 5.4*

Blessed be the God and Father of our Lord Jesus Christ, a gentle father and the God of all consolation, who comforts us in all our sorrows, so that we offer others, in their sorrows, the consolation that we have received from God ourselves. *2 Corinthians 1.3-4*

Blessed be the God and Father of our Lord Jesus Christ! By his great mercy we have been born anew to a living hope

1

through the resurrection of Jesus Christ from the dead, and to an inheritance which is imperishable, undefiled, and unfading, kept in heaven for you. *1 Peter 1.3-4*

INTRODUCTORY PRAYER

One of these prayers is used.

1 O God, Lord of life and conquerer of death, our help in every time of trouble, comfort us who mourn, and give us grace, in the presence of death, to worship you, that we may have sure hope of eternal life and be enabled to put our whole trust in your goodness and mercy; through Jesus Christ our Lord. **Amen.**

2 Eternal God our heavenly Father, who lovest us with an everlasting love, and canst turn the shadow of death into the morning; help us now to wait upon thee with reverent and submissive hearts. In the silence of this hour speak to us of eternal things, that through patience and comfort of the scriptures we may have hope, and be lifted above our dark-ness and distress into the light and peace of thy presence; through Jesus Christ our Lord. **Amen.**

3 Heavenly Father,
in your Son Jesus Christ
you have given us a true faith and a sure hope.
Help us to believe in the communion of saints,
the forgiveness of sins,
and the resurrection to eternal life;
through your Son Jesus Christ our Lord. **Amen.**

4 O gracious Lord, enable us to listen lovingly to your word.
May we console each other with the message you proclaim,

so finding light in darkness and faith in the midst of doubt; through Jesus Christ our Lord. **Amen.**

THE MINISTRY OF THE WORD

One of the following Psalms may be used as a reading or said responsively.

PSALM 23

The Lord is my shepherd:
therefore can I lack nothing.

He will make me lie down in green pastures:
and lead me beside still waters.

He will refresh my soul:
and guide me in right pathways for his name's sake.

Though I walk through the valley of the shadow of death,
    I will fear no evil:
for you are with me,
    your rod and your staff comfort me.

You spread a table before me
    in the face of those who trouble me:
you have anointed my head with oil,
    and my cup will be full.

Surely your goodness and loving-kindness
    will follow me all the days of my life:
and I shall dwell in the house of the Lord for ever.

PSALM 90. 1-6, 10, 12

Lord, you have been our refuge:
from one generation to another.

Before the mountains were born
  or the earth and the world were brought to be:
from eternity to eternity you are God.

You turn man back into dust:
saying 'Return to dust, you sons of Adam.'

For a thousand years in your sight
  are like yesterday passing:
or like one watch of the night.

You cut them short like a dream:
like the fresh grass of the morning;

In the morning it is green and flourishes:
at evening it is withered and dried up.

The days of our life are three score years and ten:
or if we have strength, four score.

Teach us so to number our days:
that we may apply our hearts to wisdom.

PSALM 121

I lift up my eyes to the hills:
but where shall I find help?

My help comes from the Lord:
who has made heaven and earth.

He will not suffer your foot to stumble:
and he who watches over you will not sleep.

Be sure he who has charge of Israel:
will neither slumber nor sleep.

The Lord himself is your keeper:
the Lord is your defence upon your right hand;

The sun shall not strike you by day:
nor shall the moon by night.

The Lord will defend you from all evil:
it is he who will guard your life.

The Lord will defend your going out and your coming in:
from this time forward for evermore.

The following are also suitable: 39.4-8, 12; 42.1-7; 103.8-18;
118.14-21, 28-29; 130.1-5, 7b.

One or more of the following Scripture passages or any other
scriptural passages in this book is read.

READINGS FROM THE OLD TESTAMENT

Isaiah 25.8-9 ; 26.3-4

The Lord God will swallow up death for ever; he will wipe
away tears from all faces, and the reproach of his people he will
take away from all the earth; for the Lord has spoken. It will
be said on that day, 'Lo, this is our God; we have waited for
him, that he might save us. This is the Lord; we have waited
for him; let us be glad and rejoice in his salvation.'

Thou dost keep him in perfect peace, whose mind is stayed on
thee, because he trusts in thee. Trust in the Lord for ever, for
the Lord God is an everlasting rock.

Lamentations 3.22-26 ; 31-33

The steadfast love of the Lord never ceases, his compassion
never fails: every morning they are renewed. so great is
his faithfulness. 'The Lord is my portion', says my soul,
'therefore I will hope in him.'

5

The Lord is good to those who wait for him, to the soul that seeks him.

It is good to wait quietly for the salvation of the Lord. For the Lord will not cast off his servants for ever; but though he causes grief, he will have compassion in the abundance of his steadfast love; for he does not willingly afflict or punish the sons of men.

READINGS FROM THE EPISTLES

Romans 8.18, 28, 35, 37-39

I consider that the sufferings of this present time are not worth comparing with the glory that is to be revealed to us.

We know that in everything God works for good with those who love him, who are called according to his purpose.

Who shall separate us from the love of Christ? Shall tribulation, or distress, or persecution, or famine, or nakedness, or peril, or sword?

No, in all these things we are more than conquerors through him who loved us. For I am sure that neither death, nor life, nor angels, nor principalities, nor things present, nor things to come, nor powers, nor height, nor depth, nor anything else in all creation, will be able to separate us from the love of God in Christ Jesus our Lord.

Romans 14.7-12

No one of us lives, and equally no one of us dies, for himself alone. If we live, we live for the Lord; and if we die, we die for the Lord. Whether therefore we live or die, we belong to the Lord. This is why Christ died and came to life again, to establish his lordship over dead and living. You, sir, why do

you pass judgement on your brother? And you, sir, why do
you hold your brother in contempt? We shall all stand before
God's tribunal. For Scripture says, 'As I live, says the Lord, to
me every knee shall bow and every tongue acknowledge God.'
So, you see, each of us will have to answer for himself.

1 Corinthians 15.19-23, 35-38, 42-44, 50, 53-55, 57-58

If in this life we who are in Christ have only hope, we are of all
men most to be pitied. But in fact Christ has been raised from
the dead, the first fruits of those who have fallen asleep. For as
by a man came death, by a man has come also the resurrection
of the dead. For as in Adam all die, so also in Christ shall all be
made alive. But each in his own order: Christ, the first fruits,
then at his coming those who belong to Christ.

But some one will ask, 'How are the dead raised? With what
kind of body do they come?' You foolish man! What you sow
does not come to life unless it dies. And what you sow is not
the body which is to be, but a bare kernel, perhaps of wheat or
of some other grain. But God gives it a body as he has chosen,
and to each kind of seed its own body.

So it is with the resurrection of the dead. What is sown is
perishable, what is raised is imperishable. It is sown in
dishonour, it is raised in glory. It is sown in weakness, it is
raised in power.

I tell you this, brethren: flesh and blood cannot inherit the
kingdom of God, nor does the perishable inherit the
imperishable.

For this perishable nature must put on the imperishable, and
this mortal nature must put on immortality. When the
perishable puts on the imperishable, and the mortal puts on
immortality, then shall come to pass the saying that is written:

'Death is swallowed up in victory.
O death, where is thy victory?
O death, where is thy sting?'
But thanks be to God, who gives us the victory through our
Lord Jesus Christ.

Therefore, my beloved brethren, be steadfast, immovable,
always abounding in the work of the Lord, knowing that in
the Lord your labour is not in vain.

Revelation 21.1-4 : 22.3-5

Then I saw a new heaven and a new earth; the first heaven
and the first earth had disappeared now, and there was no
longer any sea. I saw the holy city, and the new Jerusalem,
coming down from God out of heaven, as beautiful as a bride
all dressed for her husband. Then I heard a loud voice call
from the throne, 'You see this city? Here God lives among
men. He will make his home among them; they shall be his
people, and he will be their God; his name is God-with-them.
He will wipe away all tears from their eyes; there will be no
more death, and no more mourning or sadness. The world of
the past has gone.'

The throne of God and of the Lamb will be in its place in the
city; his servants will worship him, they will see him face to
face, and his name will be written on their foreheads. It will
never be night again and they will not need lamplight or
sunlight, because the Lord God will be shining on them. They
will reign for ever and ever.

2 Cor. 4.7-18; 2 Cor. 5.1-10
These can be used as separate readings or as one reading.

1 Thess. 4.13, 14, 18; 1 Thess. 5.1-2, 4-5, 8-11, 23;
Rev. 7.9-17; Rev. 21.1-7; Rev. 22.1-5

READINGS FROM THE GOSPELS

John 6.37-40

'All that the Father gives me will come to me; and him who comes to me I will not cast out. For I have come down from heaven, not to do my own will, but the will of him who sent me; and this is the will of him who sent me, that I should lose nothing of all that he has given me, but raise it up at the last day. For this is the will of my Father, that every one who sees the Son and believes in him should have eternal life; and I will raise him up at the last day.'

John 14.1-6, 27

'Let not your hearts be troubled; believe in God, believe also in me. In my Father's house are many rooms; if it were not so, would I have told you that I go to prepare a place for you? And when I go and prepare a place for you, I will come again and will take you to myself, that where I am you may be also. And you know the way where I am going.' Thomas said to him, 'Lord, we do not know where you are going; how can we know the way?' Jesus said to him, 'I am the way, and the truth, and the life; no one comes to the Father, but by me.

Peace I leave with you; my peace I give unto you; not as the world gives do I give you. Let not your hearts be troubled, neither let them be afraid.'

A SERMON may be given.

Here may follow the COMMUNION SERVICE.

If there is no Communion A HYMN may be sung, and the service proceeds as follows.

THE PRAYERS

One to be taken from each of the following groups, concluding with the Lord's Prayer.

A *Thanksgiving for the victory of Christ*

1 Praise and honour, glory and thanks be given to you, Almighty God, our Father, because in your great love for the world you gave your Son to be our Saviour, to live our life, to bear our griefs, and to die our death upon the Cross.

We praise you because you have brought him back from death with great power and glory, and given him all authority in heaven and on earth.

We thank you because he has conquered sin and death for us, and opened the kingdom of heaven to all believers.

We praise you for the great company of the faithful whom Christ has brought through death to behold your face in glory, who join with us in worship, prayer, and service.

For your full, perfect, and sufficient gift of life in Christ, all praise and thanks be given to you for ever and ever. **Amen.**

2 God of all grace, who didst send thy Son our Saviour Jesus Christ to bring life and immortality to light; we give thee thanks, that by his death he destroyed the power of death, and by his glorious resurrection opened the kingdom of heaven to all believers.

Grant us assuredly to know that because he lives we shall live also, and that neither death nor life, nor things present nor things to come, shall be able to separate us from thy love, which is in Christ Jesus our Lord. **Amen.**

3 We thank you, Father, that you sent your Son Jesus Christ
to die for us and to rise again.

His cross declares your love to be without limit; his
resurrection declares that death, our last enemy, is
overthrown.

By his victory we are assured of the promise that you will
never leave us or forsake us; that neither death nor life, nor
things present nor things to come, can separate us from
your love, which is in Christ Jesus our Lord. **Amen.**

4 Te Deum

You, Christ, are the King of glory:
the eternal Son of the Father.

When you became man to set us free:
you did not abhor the Virgin's womb.

You overcame the sting of death:
and opened the kingdom of heaven to all believers.

You are seated at God's right hand in glory:
We believe that you will come, and be our judge.

Come then, Lord, and help your people:
bought with the price of your own blood;

and bring us with your saints:
to glory everlasting.

B *The Commendation*

Let us then entrust our *brother* N to the mercy of God our
maker and redeemer.

1 O God, before whose face the generations rise and pass

away, we praise thy name for all thy servants departed this life in thy faith and fear, and especially for thy servant *N*.

We thank thee for all thy goodness and loving kindness to *him* throughout the days of *his* earthly life: for all that *he* was and for all that *he* accomplished by thy grace; and that now for *him* sorrow and sickness are no more, and death is past, and that *he* lives for ever in thy love and care.

Grant that, encouraged by the example of thy saints, we may run with patience the race that is set before us, looking unto Jesus, the author and finisher of our faith, so that at the last we may be one with those we love in thy presence, where there is fullness of joy; through Jesus Christ our Lord. **Amen.**

2 All-merciful Father, we give thanks for the witness of your faithful people in all generations. Especially we give thanks for all by which *N* is remembered: for all that *he* was to those who loved *him*; and for everything in *his* life that reflected your mercy and love.

We thank you that for *him* sickness and sorrow are no more and that *he* is at rest with you.

And we pray for ourselves that, throwing off the sin which clings to us so easily, we may run with resolution the race that is set before us, looking to Jesus the pioneer and perfecter of our faith; so that, at the last, we may come, with all whom we have loved, to that abiding city where you reign, in which there is no death, no mourning and no sadness, for these have passed away; through Jesus Christ our Lord. **Amen.**

3 Heavenly Father, by thy mighty power thou gavest us life, and in thy love thou hast given us new life in Christ Jesus.

We now entrust *N* to thy merciful keeping; in the faith of
Jesus Christ thy Son our Lord, who died and rose again to
save us, and is now alive and reigneth with thee and the
Holy Spirit in glory for ever. **Amen.**

C *Prayers for those who mourn*

1 Father of mercies and God of all comfort, look in thy tender
love and pity, we beseech thee, on thy sorrowing servants.
Enable them to find in thee their refuge and strength, a very
present help in trouble, and to know the love of Christ,
which passes all understanding. Grant them faith and hope
in him who by death has conquered death, and by rising
again has opened the gates of everlasting life; even Jesus
Christ our Lord. **Amen.**

2 God of hope and giver of all comfort, we commend to your
tender care those who mourn the loss of loved ones. Give
them the peace that passes all understanding, and make
them to know that neither death nor life can separate them
from your love in Jesus Christ our Lord. **Amen.**

3 Almighty God, Lord of life and vanquisher of death, we
praise you for the sure hope of eternal life you have given us
in the resurrection of our Lord Jesus Christ: and we pray
that all who mourn the loss of those dear to them may enter
into his victory and know his peace; for his name's sake.
Amen.

4 Father of all mercies and God of all comfort, who madest
nothing in vain, and lovest all that thou hast made: look in
thy tender pity on thy bereaved servants, and enable them
by thy grace to find in thee their refuge and their strength;
through Jesus Christ our Lord. **Amen.**

5 Almighty God, Father of all mercies and giver of all
comfort, deal graciously, we pray you, with those who

mourn, that casting all their care on you they may know the consolation of your love; through Jesus Christ our Lord. **Amen.**

or

Our Father in heaven,
hallowed be your name,
your kingdom come,
your will be done,
on earth as in heaven.
Give us today our daily
bread.
Forgive us our sins
as we forgive those
who sin against us.
Lead us not into
temptation
but deliver us from evil.

For the kingdom, the
power, and the glory are
yours
now and for ever. Amen.

Our Father, which art in
heaven,
Hallowed be thy name;
Thy kingdom come;
Thy will be done;
In earth as it is in heaven.
Give us this day our daily
bread.
And forgive us our
trespasses,
As we forgive them that
trespass against us.
And lead us not into
temptation;
But deliver us from evil.

For thine is the kingdom,
the power,
and the glory,
for ever and ever. Amen.

DECLARATION OF COMMITTAL AND ENTRUSTMENT

When the whole Service takes place in a crematorium chapel the Committal follows; but if the Committal is to take place elsewhere, a hymn may be sung, and the Service ends with this sentence and a blessing.

Now may the God of peace who brought again from the dead our Lord Jesus, the great shepherd of the sheep, by the blood of the eternal covenant, equip you with everything good that you may do his will, working in you that which is pleasing in

14

his sight, through Jesus Christ, to whom be glory for ever and ever. **Amen.** *Hebrews 13.20-21*

COMMITTAL

One or more of the following sentences is said at the grave or at the crematorium.

I am the resurrection and the life, says the Lord: he who believes in me, though he die, yet shall he live, and whoever lives and believes in me shall never die. *John 11.25-26*

Whether we live, we live to the Lord, and whether we die, we die to the Lord; so then, whether we live, or whether we die, we are the Lord's. For to this end Christ died and lived again, that he might be Lord both of the dead and of the living. *Romans 14.8-9*

Do not be afraid. I am the first and the last, says the Lord, and I am the living one; for I was dead and now I am alive for evermore, and I hold the keys of Death and Death's domain. *Revelation 1.17b-18a*

At the grave

Having commended into the hands of God our *brother* departed, we now commit *his* body to the ground, earth to earth, ashes to ashes, dust to dust; putting our whole trust and confidence in the mercy of our heavenly Father, and in the victory of his Son, Jesus Christ our Lord, who died, was buried, and rose again for us, and is alive and reigns for ever and ever. **Amen.**

At the crematorium

Having commended into the hands of God our *brother* departed, we now commit *his* body to be cremated, ashes to

15

ashes, dust to dust; putting our whole trust and confidence in the mercy of our heavenly Father, and in the victory of his Son, Jesus Christ our Lord, who died, was buried, and rose again for us, and is alive and reigns for ever and ever. **Amen.**

At sea

Having commended into the hands of God our *brother* departed, we now commit *his* body to the deep; putting our whole trust and confidence in the mercy of our heavenly Father, and in the victory of his Son, Jesus Christ our Lord, who died, was buried, and rose again for us, and is alive and reigns for ever and ever. **Amen.**

Then may be said

I heard a voice from heaven, saying, 'Write this: Happy are the dead who die in the faith of Christ! Henceforth, says the Spirit, they may rest from their labours; for they take with them the record of their deeds.'

Then is said one of the following prayers.

O God, maker and redeemer of all mankind, grant to us with your servant *N* and all the faithful departed, the sure benefits of your Son's saving passion and glorious resurrection; that in the last day, when you gather up all things in Christ, we may with them enjoy the fullness of your promises; through Jesus Christ our Lord. **Amen.**

Hear, Lord, the prayers of your people, as we remember before you *N* our *brother*; and grant that we who confess your name on earth may with *him* be made perfect in the kingdom of your glory; through Jesus Christ our Lord. **Amen.**

Remember, O Lord, this servant, who has gone before us with the sign of faith, and now rests in the sleep of peace. According to your promises, grant to *him* and all who rest in Christ, refreshment, light, and peace; through Jesus Christ our Lord. **Amen.**

Father of all, by whose mercy and grace your saints remain in everlasting light and peace: we remember with thanksgiving those whom we love but see no longer; and we pray that in them your perfect will may be fulfilled; through Jesus Christ our Lord. **Amen.**

Unto him that is able to keep us from falling, and to present us faultless before the presence of his glory with exceeding joy, to the only wise God our Saviour, be glory and majesty, dominion and power, both now and for ever. **Amen.**
Jude 24-25

The Disposal of Ashes

The service begins with a sentence from the previous services or the following:

Either

Now is Christ risen from the dead, and become the first fruits of them that slept.

or

Christ has been raised from the dead, the first fruits of those who have fallen asleep.

Having commended our *brother* N to the care of God our maker and redeemer, we now commit *his* ashes to this place, earth to earth, dust to dust; putting our whole trust and confidence in the mercy of our heavenly Father, and in the victory of his Son, Jesus Christ our Lord, who died, was buried, and rose again for us, and is alive and reigns for ever and ever. **Amen.**

Let us pray.

Either

Almighty God, grant that we, with all those who have believed in thee, may be united in the full knowledge of thy love and the unclouded vision of thy glory; through Jesus Christ our Lord. **Amen.**

or

Almighty God, grant that we, with all those who have believed in you, may be united in the full knowledge of your love and the unclouded vision of your glory; through Jesus Christ our Lord. **Amen.**

The grace of our Lord Jesus Christ, and the love of God, and the fellowship of the Holy Spirit be with us all evermore. **Amen.**

If pastoral needs require, additional material may be used at the Disposal of the Ashes.

The Funeral of a Child

On these occasions the following material may be used instead of the provision in the earlier Funeral Service.

INTRODUCTORY SENTENCES

He shall feed his flock like a shepherd. He shall gather the lambs with his arm, and carry them in his bosom. *Isaiah 40.11*

As one whom his mother comforts, so will I comfort you, says the Lord. *Isaiah 66.13*

Blessed are those who mourn, for they shall be comforted. *Matthew 5.4*

I am the resurrection and the life, says the Lord; he who believes in me, though he die, yet shall he live, and whoever lives and believes in me shall never die. *John 11.25-26*

READINGS

One of the following:

Psalm 23 (see page 3); 2 Corinthians 1.3-4; Matthew 18.2-5, 10, 14; Mark 10.13-16; Revelation 21.4; John 14.1-6, 18-19, 27

COMMENDATION

Almighty God, whose kingdom we cannot receive unless we be as children, we thank you for the gift of this little child. We thank you for the love and trust which *he* inspired in the hearts of those to whom *he* came: for the joy which *he* has given to all who knew *him* and for the precious memories of *him* that will abide.

Father, as your Son took little children into his arms and blessed them, take this little one into your safe keeping now and for ever.

Father in heaven, healer of broken hearts, we ask you to look in pity and compassion upon your servants whose joy has been turned into mourning. Comfort them and grant that they may be drawn closer to each other by their common sorrow. Dwell with them and be their refuge until the day break and the shadows flee away; through Jesus Christ our Lord. **Amen.**

COMMITTAL

Jesus said,
Let the children come to me, do not hinder them; for to such belongs the Kingdom of God.

It is not the will of my Father who is in heaven that one of these little ones shall perish.

At the grave

Having commended this child N to the care of God our maker and redeemer, we now commit *his* body to the ground, earth to earth, ashes to ashes, dust to dust; putting our whole trust and confidence in the mercy of our heavenly Father, and in the victory of his Son, Jesus Christ our Lord, who died, was buried, and rose again for us, and is alive and reigns for ever and ever. **Amen.**

At the crematorium

Having commended this child N to the care of God our maker and redeemer, we now commit *his* body to be cremated, ashes to ashes, dust to dust; putting our whole trust and confidence in the mercy of our heavenly Father, and in the victory of his

Son, Jesus Christ our Lord, who died, was buried, and rose again for us, and is alive and reigns for ever and ever. **Amen.**

These prayers follow

O God, in whose mighty power it lies to bring good out of evil, and to raise up life from the dead; grant us a patient faith in time of darkness, and enlighten our understanding with the knowledge of your ways; through Jesus Christ our Lord. **Amen.**

Unto him that is able to keep us from falling, and to present us faultless before the presence of his glory with exceeding joy, to the only wise God our Saviour, be glory and majesty, dominion and power, both now and for ever. **Amen.**
Jude 24-25

Funeral Service
(Modern Language)
Church of England

The Service for the Funeral of a Child is not printed separately,
but the appropriate paragraphs are indicated by two green
asterisks **. This does not exclude the use of other material.

Stand

Minister   Jesus said, I am the resurrection, and I am the life;
he who believes in me, though he die, yet shall he
live, and whoever lives and believes in me shall
never die. *John 11.25-26*

He may add one or more of these or other SENTENCES OF
SCRIPTURE.

We brought nothing into the world, and we take nothing out.
The Lord gives, and the Lord takes away: blessed be the name
of the Lord. *1 Timothy 6.7 ; Job 1.21*

The eternal God is your refuge, and underneath are the
everlasting arms. *Deuteronomy 33.27*

The steadfast love of the Lord never ceases, his compassion
never fails: every morning they are renewed.
Lamentations 3.22-23

Blessed are those who mourn, for they shall be comforted.
Matthew 5.4

God so loved the world that he gave his only Son, that
whoever believes in him should not perish, but have eternal
life. *John 3.16*

I am sure that neither death, nor life, nor angels, nor principalities, nor powers, nor things present, nor things to come, nor height, nor depth, nor anything else in all creation, will be able to separate us from the love of God in Christ Jesus our Lord. *Romans 8.38-39*

Eye has not seen, nor ear heard, nor the heart of man conceived, what God has prepared for those who love him. *1 Corinthians 2.9*

We believe that Jesus died and rose again; and so it will be for those who died as Christians; God will bring them to life with Jesus. Thus we shall always be with the Lord. Comfort one another with these words. *1 Thessalonians 4.14, 18*

The following is suitable at the funeral of a child. Others from the above could be used also.

**The Lamb who is at the throne will be their shepherd and will lead them to springs of living water; and God will wipe away all tears from their eyes. *Revelation 7.17*

Minister   Heavenly Father,
in your Son Jesus Christ
you have given us a true faith and
a sure hope.
Strengthen this faith and hope in us
all our days,
that we may live as those who believe in
the communion of saints,
the forgiveness of sins,
and the resurrection to eternal life;
through your Son Jesus Christ our Lord.
    Amen.

24

One or both of the following PSALMS are said

** PSALM 23

1 The Lord is my shepherd :
   therefore can I lack nothing.

2 He will make me lie down in green pastures :
   and lead me beside still waters.

3 He will refresh my soul :
   and guide me in right pathways for his name's sake.

4 Though I walk through the valley of the shadow of death,
     I will fear no evil :
   for you are with me,
     your rod and your staff comfort me.

5 You spread a table before me
     in the face of those who trouble me :
   you have anointed my head with oil,
     and my cup will be full.

6 Surely your goodness and loving-kindness
     will follow me all the days of my life :
   and I shall dwell in the house of the Lord for ever.

   Glory to the Father, and to the Son,
     and to the Holy Spirit,
   as it was in the beginning, is now,
     and shall be for ever. Amen.

   Verses from PSALM 90

1 Lord, you have been our refuge :
   from one generation to another.

25

2 Before the mountains were born
  or the earth and the world were brought to be:
from eternity to eternity you are God.

3 You turn man back into dust:
saying 'Return to dust, you sons of Adam.'

4 For a thousand years in your sight
  are like yesterday passing:
or like one watch of the night.

5 You cut them short like a dream:
like the fresh grass of the morning;

6 In the morning it is green and flourishes:
at evening it is withered and dried up.

10 The days of our life are three score years and ten,
  or if we have strength, four score:
the pride of our labours is but toil and sorrow,
  for it passes quickly away and we are gone.

12 Teach us so to number our days:
that we may apply our hearts to wisdom.

14 O satisfy us early with your mercy:
that all our days we may rejoice and sing.

16 Show your servants your work:
and let their children see your glory.

17 May the gracious favour of the Lord our God
  be upon us:
prosper the work of our hands,
  O prosper the work of our hands!

Glory to the Father, and to the Son,
  and to the Holy Spirit:
as it was in the beginning, is now,
  and shall be for ever. Amen.

Sit

One or more of the following READINGS

John 14.1-6 JB
Jesus said to his disciples,
'Do not let your hearts be troubled.
Trust in God still, and trust in me.
There are many rooms in my Father's house;
if there were not, I should have told you.
I am going now to prepare a place for you,
and after I have gone and prepared you a place,
I shall return to take you with me;
so that where I am
you may be too.
You know the way to the place where I am going.'

Thomas said, 'Lord, we do not know where you are going,
so how can we know the way?' Jesus said,

'I am the Way, the Truth and the Life.
No one can come to the Father except through me.'

1 Corinthians 15.20-26, 35-38, 42-44a, 53-end RSV
Christ has been raised from the dead, the first fruits of those
who have fallen asleep. For as by a man came death, by a man
has come also the resurrection of the dead. For as in Adam all
die, so also in Christ shall all be made alive. But each in his
own order: Christ the first fruits, then at his coming those who
belong to Christ. Then comes the end, when he delivers the
kingdom to God the Father after destroying every rule and
every authority and power. For he must reign until he has put
all his enemies under his feet. The last enemy to be destroyed
is death.

But someone will ask, 'How are the dead raised? With what
kind of body do they come?' You foolish man! What you sow

does not come to life unless it dies. And what you sow is not the body which is to be, but a bare kernel, perhaps of wheat or of some other grain. But God gives it a body as he has chosen, and to each kind of seed its own body.

So it is with the resurrection of the dead. What is sown is perishable, what is raised is imperishable. It is sown in dishonour, it is raised in glory. It is sown in weakness, it is raised in power. It is sown a physical body, it is raised a spiritual body.

For this perishable nature must put on the imperishable, and this mortal nature must put on immortality. When the perishable puts on the imperishable, and the mortal puts on immortality, then shall come to pass the saying that is written: 'Death is swallowed up in victory.' 'O death, where is thy victory? O death, where is thy sting?' The sting of death is sin, and the power of sin is the law. But thanks be to God, who gives us the victory through our Lord Jesus Christ.

Therefore, my beloved brethren, be steadfast, immovable, always abounding in the work of the Lord, knowing that in the Lord your labour is not in vain.

✶✶*Mark 10.13-16 NEB*
They brought children for Jesus to touch. The disciples rebuked them, but when Jesus saw this he was indignant, and said to them, 'Let the children come to me; do not try to stop them; for the kingdom of God belongs to such as these. I tell you, whoever does not accept the kingdom of God like a child will never enter it.' And he put his arms round them, laid his hands upon them, and blessed them.

ALTERNATIVE READINGS: Wisdom 4.8, 10-11, 13-15; John 5.19-25; John 6.35-40; John 11.17-27; Romans 8.31b-39; Romans 14.7-9; 2 Corinthians 1.3-5; 2 Corinthians 4.7-18;

Philippians 3.10-end; 1 Thessalonians 4.13-18; Revelation 21.1-7

A SERMON may be preached.

Stand
Verses from TE DEUM, or A HYMN

You, Christ, are the King of glory:
the eternal Son of the Father.

When you became man to set us free:
you did not abhor the Virgin's womb.

You overcame the sting of death:
and opened the kingdom of heaven to all believers.

You are seated at God's right hand in glory:
we believe that you will come and be our judge.

Come then Lord and help your people:
bought with the price of your own blood;

and bring us with your saints:
to glory everlasting.

★★Minister   Let us pray.

Lord, have mercy upon us.
All   Christ, have mercy upon us.
Minister   Lord, have mercy upon us.

All	Our Father in heaven,	or	Our Father, who art in heaven,
	hallowed be your name,		hallowed be thy name;
	your kingdom come,		thy kingdom come;
	your will be done,		thy will be done;
	on earth as in heaven.		on earth as it is in heaven.

Give us today our daily bread.
Forgive us our sins
as we forgive those
    who sin against us.
Lead us not into temptation
but deliver us from evil.
	Give us this day our daily bread.
	And forgive us our trespasses,
	as we forgive those
	    who trespass against us.
	And lead us not into temptation;
	but deliver us from evil.

For the kingdom, the power,
    and the glory are yours
now and for ever. Amen.
	For thine is the kingdom,
	    the power, and the glory,
	for ever and ever. Amen.

PRAYERS may be said here (see pages 34–35).

Minister Grant us, Lord, the wisdom and the grace to use aright the time that is left to us here on earth. Lead us to repent of our sins, the evil we have done and the good we have not done; and strengthen us to follow the steps of your Son, in the way that leads to the fullness of eternal life; through Jesus Christ our Lord. **Amen.

A HYMN may be sung.

**Minister Let us commend our *brother N* or this *child N* to the mercy of God our Maker and Redeemer.

Heavenly Father, by your mighty power you gave us life, and in your love you have given us new life in Christ Jesus. We entrust *N* to your merciful keeping, in the faith of Jesus Christ your Son our Lord, who died and rose again to save us, and is now alive and reigns with you and the Holy Spirit in glory for ever. **Amen.**

The Committal follows. For a longer form of the Committal see page 32.

** We have entrusted our *brother N* or this *child N* to God's merciful keeping, and we now commit *his* body to be cremated (*or* to the ground): *[earth to earth, ashes to ashes, dust to dust;] in sure and certain hope of the resurrection to eternal life through our Lord Jesus Christ, who died, was buried, and rose again for us. To him be glory for ever and ever.

God will show us the path of life; in his presence is the fullness of joy: and at his right hand there is pleasure for evermore. *Psalm 16.11*

** Unto him that is able to keep us from falling, and to present us faultless before the presence of his glory with exceeding joy, to the only wise God our Saviour, be glory and majesty, dominion and power, both now and ever. **Amen.** *Jude 24-25*

or

** May God in his infinite love and mercy bring the whole Church, living and departed in the Lord Jesus, to a joyful resurrection and the fulfilment of his eternal kingdom. **Amen.**

* The words in square brackets may be omitted.

The Committal

For use before or after a Service in Church
The minister may say

I heard a voice from heaven, saying, 'Write this: "Happy are the dead who die in the faith of Christ! Henceforth, says the Spirit, they may rest from their labours; for they take with them the record of their deeds."' *Revelation 14.13*

**Verses from PSALM 103

The Lord is full of compassion and mercy:
slow to anger and of great goodness.
As a father is tender towards his children:
so is the Lord tender to those that fear him.
For he knows of what we are made:
he remembers that we are but dust.
The days of man are but as grass:
he flourishes like a flower of the field;
when the wind goes over it, it is gone:
and its place will know it no more.
But the merciful goodness of the Lord
endures for ever and ever toward those that fear him:
and his righteousness upon their children's children.

or

Man born of a woman has but a short time to live. Like a flower he blossoms and then withers; like a shadow he flees and never stays.

In the midst of life we are in death; to whom can we turn for help, but to you, Lord, who are justly angered by our sins?

Lord God, holy and mighty, holy and immortal, holy and most merciful Saviour, deliver us from the bitter pains of eternal death. You know the secrets of our hearts: in your mercy hear our prayer, forgive us our sins, and at our last hour let us not fall away from you.

The minister then says

**We have entrusted [our *brother* or this *child*] N to God's merciful keeping, and we now commit *his* body to be cremated (or to the ground): *[earth to earth, ashes to ashes, dust to dust;] in sure and certain hope of the resurrection to eternal life through our Lord Jesus Christ, who died, was buried, and rose again for us. To him be glory for ever and ever.

God will show us the path of life;
in his presence is the fullness of joy:
and at his right hand
there is pleasure for evermore. *Psalm 16.11*

Unto him that is able to keep us from falling, and to present us faultless before the presence of his glory with exceeding joy, to the only wise God our Saviour, be glory and majesty, dominion and power, both now and ever. **Amen. *Jude 24-25*

or

May God in his infinite love and mercy bring the whole Church, living and departed in the Lord Jesus, to a joyful resurrection and the fulfilment of his eternal kingdom. **Amen.

* The words in square brackets may be omitted.

A Selection of Prayers which may be used

Merciful Father and Lord of all life, we praise you that men are made in your image and reflect your truth and light. We thank you for the life of your *son N*, for the love and mercy *he* received from you and showed among us. Above all we rejoice at your gracious promise to all your servants, living and departed: that we shall rise again at the coming of Christ. And we ask that in due time we may share with our *brother* that clearer vision, when we shall see your face in the same Christ our Lord. **Amen.**

O God, the maker and redeemer of all mankind: grant us, with your servant *N* and all the faithful departed, the sure benefits of your Son's saving passion and glorious resurrection; that in the last day, when you gather up all things in Christ, we may with them enjoy the fullness of your promise; through Jesus Christ our Lord. **Amen.**

Hear, Lord, the prayers of your people, as we remember before you *N* our *brother*; and grant that we who confess your name on earth may with *him* be made perfect in the kingdom of your glory; through Jesus Christ our Lord. **Amen.**

Remember, O Lord, this your servant, who has gone before us with the sign of faith, and now rests in the sleep of peace. According to your promises, grant to *him* and to all who rest in Christ, refreshment, light, and peace; through the same Christ our Lord. **Amen.**

Eternal Lord God, you hold all souls in life: shed forth, we pray, upon your whole Church in paradise and on earth the bright beams of your light and heavenly comfort; and grant that we, following the good example of those who have loved and served you here and are now at rest, may at the last enter with them into the fullness of your eternal joy; through Jesus Christ our Lord. **Amen.**

The following prayer is suitable at the funeral of a child.

** Father in heaven, you gave your Son Jesus Christ to suffering and to death on the cross, and raised him to life in glory. Grant us a patient faith in time of darkness, and strengthen our hearts with the knowledge of your love; through Jesus Christ our Lord. **Amen.**

Father of all, by whose mercy and grace your saints remain in everlasting light and peace: we remember with thanksgiving those whom we love but see no longer; and we pray that in them your perfect will may be fulfilled; through Jesus Christ our Lord. **Amen.**

Almighty God, Father of all mercies and giver of all comfort: deal graciously, we pray, with those who mourn, that casting all their care on you, they may know the consolation of your love; through Jesus Christ our Lord. **Amen.**

O Lord, support us all the day long of this troublous life, until the shades lengthen, and the evening comes, and the busy world is hushed, the fever of life is over, and our work done. Then, Lord, in your mercy grant us safe lodging, a holy rest, and peace at the last; through Jesus Christ our Lord. **Amen.**

Funeral Service
(Traditional Language)
Church of England

*The Service for the Funeral of a Child is not printed separately,
but the appropriate paragraphs are indicated by two green
asterisks **. This does not exclude the use of other material.*

THE INTRODUCTION

The Ministers meeting the body at the entrance and going
before it shall say one or more of the following sentences.

I am the resurrection and the life, saith the Lord: he that
believeth in me, though he were dead, yet shall he live; and
whosoever liveth and believeth in me shall never die.
St John 11.25-26

I know that my Redeemer liveth, and that he shall stand up at
the last upon the earth: whom I shall see for myself, and mine
eyes shall behold, and not another. *Job 19.25-27*

We brought nothing into this world, and it is certain we can
carry nothing out. The Lord gave, and the Lord hath taken
away; blessed be the name of the Lord. *1 Timothy 6.7; Job 1.21*

Remember not the sins and offences of my youth: but
according to thy mercy think thou upon me, O Lord, for thy
goodness. *Psalm 25.6*

The eternal God is thy refuge, and underneath are the
everlasting arms. *Deuteronomy 33.27*

Neither death, nor life, nor angels, nor principalities, nor
powers, nor things present, nor things to come, nor height,

nor depth, nor any other creature, shall be able to separate us from the love of God, which is in Christ Jesus our Lord. *Romans 8.38-39*

Whether we live, we live unto the Lord; and whether we die, we die unto the Lord: whether we live therefore, or die, we are the Lord's. For to this end Christ both died, and rose, and revived, that he might be Lord both of the dead and living. *Romans 14.8-9*

Blessed are they that mourn: for they shall be comforted. *St. Matthew 5.4*

Let not your heart be troubled: ye believe in God, believe also in me. In my Father's house are many mansions. *St. John 14.1*

The following is suitable at the funeral of a child.

**He shall feed his flock like a shepherd: he shall gather the lambs with his arms, and carry them in his bosom. *Isaiah 40.11*

Then shall be read one or both of these PSALMS following. At the end of all the Psalms the *Gloria Patri* may be left unsaid, and instead thereof may be sung or said

Rest eternal grant unto them, O Lord: and let light perpetual shine upon them.

Before and after any Psalm or group of Psalms may be said or sung the Anthem following.

O Saviour of the world, who by thy Cross and precious Blood hast redeemed us: Save us and help us, we humbly beseech thee, O Lord.

PSALM 90

1 Lord, thou hast been our refuge:
   from one generation to another.

2 Before the mountains were brought forth,
       or ever the earth and the world were made:
   thou art God from everlasting, and world without end.

3 Thou turnest man to destruction:
   again thou sayest, Come again, ye children of men.

4 For a thousand years in thy sight are but as yesterday:
   seeing that is past as a watch in the night.

5 As soon as thou scatterest them, they are even as a sleep:
   and fade away suddenly like the grass.

6 In the morning it is green, and groweth up:
   but in the evening it is cut down, dried up,
       and withered.

7 For we consume away in thy displeasure:
   and are afraid at thy wrathful indignation.

8 Thou hast set our misdeeds before thee:
   and our secret sins in the light of thy countenance.

9 For when thou art angry all our days are gone:
   we bring our years to an end, as it were a tale
       that is told.

10 The days of our age are threescore years and ten;
       and though men be so strong, that they come to
       fourscore years:
   yet is their strength then but labour and sorrow;
       so soon passeth it away, and we are gone.

11 But who regardeth the power of thy wrath:
for even thereafter as a man feareth,
   so is thy displeasure.

12 So teach us to number our days:
that we may apply our hearts unto wisdom.

13 Turn thee again, O Lord, at the last:
and be gracious unto thy servants.

14 O satisfy us with thy mercy, and that soon:
so shall we rejoice and be glad all the days of our life.

15 Comfort us again now after the time that thou hast
   plagued us:
and for the years wherein we have suffered adversity.

16 Shew thy servants thy work:
and their children thy glory.

17 And the glorious Majesty of the Lord our God be upon us:
prosper thou the work of our hands upon us,
   O prosper thou our handy-work.

Glory be to the Father, and to the Son:
and to the Holy Ghost;

As it was in the beginning, is now, and ever shall be:
world without end. Amen.

**PSALM 23

1 The Lord is my shepherd:
therefore can I lack nothing.

2 He shall feed me in a green pasture:
and lead me forth beside the waters of comfort.

3 He shall convert my soul:
   and bring me forth in the paths of righteousness,
      for his name's sake.

4 Yea, though I walk through the valley of the shadow
      of death, I will fear no evil:
   for thou art with me;
      thy rod and thy staff comfort me.

5 Thou shalt prepare a table before me
      against them that trouble me:
   thou hast anointed my head with oil,
      and my cup shall be full.

6 But thy loving-kindness and mercy
      shall follow me all the days of my life: and I will dwell in
   the house of the Lord for ever.

   Glory be to the Father, and to the Son:
   and to the Holy Ghost;

   As it was in the beginning, is now, and ever shall be:
   world without end. Amen.

Then shall be read the LESSON following

1 Corinthians 15.20-26, 35-38, 42-44, 53-58

Now is Christ risen from the dead, and become the first-fruits
of them that slept. For since by man came death, by man came
also the resurrection of the dead. For as in Adam all die, even
so in Christ shall all be made alive. But every man in his own
order: Christ the first-fruits; afterward they that are Christ's,
at his coming. Then cometh the end, when he shall have
delivered up the kingdom to God, even the Father; when he
shall have put down all rule, and all authority, and power. For
he must reign, till he hath put all enemies under his feet. The
last enemy that shall be destroyed is death.

But some man will say, How are the dead raised up? and with what body do they come? Thou fool, that which thou sowest is not quickened, except it die. And that which thou sowest, thou sowest not that body that shall be, but bare grain, it may chance of wheat, or of some other grain: But God giveth it a body, as it hath pleased him, and to every seed his own body. So also is the resurrection of the dead: It is sown in corruption; it is raised in incorruption: It is sown in dishonour; it is raised in glory: It is sown in weakness; it is raised in power: It is sown a natural body; it is raised a spiritual body. For this corruptible must put on incorruption, and this mortal must put on immortality. So when this corruptible shall have put on incorruption, and this mortal shall have put on immortality; then shall be brought to pass the saying that is written, Death is swallowed up in victory. O death, where is thy sting? O grave, where is thy victory? The sting of death is sin, and the strength of sin is the law. But thanks be to God, which giveth us the victory through our Lord Jesus Christ. Therefore, my beloved brethren, be ye steadfast, unmovable, always abounding in the work of the Lord, forasmuch as ye know that your labour is not in vain in the Lord.

Or at the funeral of a child

**St Mark 10.13-16*

They brought young children to him, that he should touch them: and his disciples rebuked those that brought them. But when Jesus saw it, he was much displeased, and said unto them, Suffer the little children to come unto me, and forbid them not; for of such is the kingdom of God. Verily I say unto you, Whosoever shall not receive the kingdom of God as a little child, he shall not enter therein. And he took them up in his arms, put his hands upon them, and blessed them.

ALTERNATIVE READINGS 2 Cor. 4.16—5.10; Rev. 7.4-17; Rev. 21.1-7

THE PRAYERS

Then shall the Minister say

**Let us pray.

> Lord, have mercy upon us.
> **Christ, have mercy upon us.**
> Lord, have mercy upon us.

**Our Father, which art in heaven,
Hallowed be thy name;
Thy kingdom come;
Thy will be done;
In earth as it is in heaven.
Give us this day our daily bread.
And forgive us our trespasses,
As we forgive them that trespass against us.
And lead us not into temptation;
But deliver us from evil.
Amen.**

The following VERSICLES AND RESPONSES may then be said by the Minister and People, except that at the funeral of a child the first Versicle and Response shall not be said.

Minister   Enter not into judgement with thy servant,
           O Lord;
All   **For in thy sight shall no man living be justified.**

Minister   Grant unto *him* eternal rest;
All   **And let perpetual light shine upon *him*.**

Minister   We believe verily to see the goodness of the Lord;
All   **In the land of the living.**

Minister   O Lord, hear our prayer;
All   **And let our cry come unto thee.**

Then shall be said one or more of the following PRAYERS

Almighty God, with whom do live the spirits of them that
depart hence in the Lord, and with whom the souls of the
faithful, after they are delivered from the burden of the flesh,
are in joy and felicity: We give thee hearty thanks, for that it
hath pleased thee to deliver this our *brother* out of the miseries
of this sinful world; beseeching thee, that it may please thee,
of thy gracious goodness, shortly to accomplish the number of
thine elect, and to hasten thy kingdom; that we, with all those
that are departed in the true faith of thy holy name, may have
our perfect consummation and bliss, both in body and soul, in
thy eternal and everlasting glory; through Jesus Christ our
Lord. **Amen.**

THE COLLECT

O merciful God, the Father of our Lord Jesus Christ, who is
the resurrection and the life; in whom whosoever believeth
shall live, though he die; and whosoever liveth, and believeth
in him, shall not die eternally; who also hath taught us, by his
holy Apostle Saint Paul, not to be sorry, as men without hope,
for them that sleep in him: We meekly beseech thee,
O Father, to raise us from the death of sin unto the life of
righteousness; that, when we shall depart this life, we may rest
in him, as our hope is this our *brother* doth; and that, at the
general resurrection in the last day, we may be found
acceptable in thy sight; and receive that blessing, which thy
well-beloved Son shall then pronounce to all that love and fear

44

thee, saying, Come, ye blessed children of my Father, receive the kingdom prepared for you from the beginning of the world. Grant this, we beseech thee, O merciful Father, through Jesus Christ, our Mediator and Redeemer. **Amen.**

O Father of all, we pray to thee for those whom we love, but see no longer. Grant them thy peace; let light perpetual shine upon them; and in thy loving wisdom and almighty power work in them the good purpose of thy perfect will; through Jesus Christ our Lord. **Amen.**

Almighty God, Father of all mercies and giver of all comfort: Deal graciously, we pray thee, with those who mourn, that casting every care on thee, they may know the consolation of thy love; through Jesus Christ our Lord. **Amen.**

O heavenly Father, who in thy Son Jesus Christ, hast given us a true faith, and a sure hope: Help us, we pray thee, to live as those who believe and trust in the Communion of Saints, the forgiveness of sins, and the resurrection to life everlasting, and strengthen this faith and hope in us all the days of our life: through the love of thy Son, Jesus Christ our Saviour. **Amen.**

At the funeral of a child

O Lord Jesu Christ, who didst take little children into thine arms and bless them: Open thou our eyes, we beseech thee, to perceive that it is of thy goodness that thou hast taken this thy child into the everlasting arms of thine infinite love; who livest and reignest with the Father and the Holy Spirit, ever one God, world without end. **Amen.

**O God, whose ways are hidden and thy works most wonderful, who makest nothing in vain and lovest all that thou hast made: Comfort thou thy servants, whose hearts are

45

sore smitten and oppressed; and grant that they may so love and serve thee in this life, that together with this thy child, they may obtain the fulness of thy promises in the world to come; through Jesus Christ our Lord. **Amen.**

The Committal follows. For a longer form of the Committal see page 48.

The Minister shall say

**Forasmuch as it hath pleased Almighty God of his great mercy to take unto himself the soul of our dear *brother* (or this *child*) here departed, we therefore commit *his* body to be consumed by fire (or to the ground); earth to earth, ashes to ashes, dust to dust; in sure and certain hope of the resurrection to eternal life through our Lord Jesus Christ; who shall change the body of our low estate that it may be like unto his glorious body, according to the mighty working, whereby he is able to subdue all things to himself.

Or this

We commend unto thy hands of mercy, most merciful Father, the soul of this our *brother* (or this thy *child*) departed, and we commit *his* body to be consumed by fire (or to the ground), earth to earth, ashes to ashes, dust to dust. And we beseech thine infinite goodness to give us grace to live in thy fear and love and to die in thy favour, that when the judgement shall come which thou hast committed to thy well-beloved Son, both this our *brother* (or this *child*) and we may be found acceptable in thy sight. Grant this, O merciful Father, for the sake of Jesus Christ, our only Saviour, Mediator, and Advocate. **Amen.

46

Then shall be said or sung

I heard a voice from heaven, saying unto me, Write, From henceforth blessed are the dead which die in the Lord: even so saith the Spirit; for they rest from their labours.

Or, at the funeral of a child

**They shall hunger no more, neither thirst any more; neither shall the sun light on them, nor any heat. For the Lamb which is in the midst of the throne shall feed them, and shall lead them unto living fountains of waters: and God shall wipe away all tears from their eyes.

Here may be added by the Minister

Now unto the King eternal, immortal, invisible, the only wise God, be honour and glory for ever and ever. **Amen.

or

The grace of our Lord Jesus Christ, and the love of God, and the fellowship of the Holy Ghost, be with us all evermore. **Amen.

The Committal

This Committal may be used before or after a Service in Church. The Minister shall say

Man that is born of a woman hath but a short time to live, and is full of misery. He cometh up, and is cut down, like a flower; he fleeth as it were a shadow, and never continueth in one stay.

In the midst of life we are in death: of whom may we seek for succour, but of thee, O Lord, who for our sins art justly displeased?

Yet, O Lord God most holy, O Lord most mighty, O holy and most merciful Saviour, deliver us not into the bitter pains of eternal death.

Thou knowest, Lord, the secrets of our hearts; shut not thy merciful ears to our prayer; but spare us, Lord most holy, O God most mighty, O holy and merciful Saviour, thou most worthy Judge eternal, suffer us not, at our last hour, for any pains of death, to fall from thee.

Or this

PSALM 103.13-17
Like as a father pitieth his own children:
even so is the Lord merciful unto them that fear him.
For he knoweth whereof we are made:
he remembereth that we are but dust.
The days of man are but as grass:
for he flourisheth as a flower of the field.
For as soon as the wind goeth over it, it is gone:
and the place thereof shall know it no more.

But the merciful goodness of the Lord
    endureth for ever and ever upon them that fear him:
and his righteousness upon children's children.

Then shall the Minister say

Forasmuch as it hath pleased Almighty God of his great mercy
to take unto himself the soul of our dear *brother* (or this *child*)
here departed, we therefore commit *his* body to be consumed
by fire (or to the ground), earth to earth, ashes to ashes, dust to
dust; in sure and certain hope of the resurrection to eternal life
through our Lord Jesus Christ; who shall change the body of
our low estate that it may be like unto his glorious body,
according to the mighty working, whereby he is able to
subdue all things to himself.

Or this

We commend unto thy hands of mercy, most merciful Father,
the soul of this our *brother* (or this thy *child*) departed, and we
commit *his* body to be consumed by fire (or to the ground),
earth to earth, ashes to ashes, dust to dust. And we beseech
thine infinite goodness to give us grace to live in thy fear and
love and to die in thy favour, that when the judgement shall
come which thou hast committed to thy well-beloved Son,
both this our *brother* (or this *child*) and we may be found
acceptable in thy sight. Grant this, O merciful Father, for the
sake of Jesus Christ, our only Saviour, Mediator, and
Advocate. **Amen.**

Then shall be said or sung

I heard a voice from heaven, saying unto me, Write, From
henceforth blessed are the dead which die in the Lord: even so
saith the Spirit; for they rest from their labours.

Or at the funeral of a child

**They shall hunger no more, neither thirst any more; neither shall the sun light on them, nor any heat. For the Lamb which is in the midst of the throne shall feed them, and shall lead them unto living fountains of waters: and God shall wipe away all tears from their eyes.

Here shall be added by the Minister

Now unto the King eternal, immortal, invisible, the only wise God, be honour and glory for ever and ever. **Amen.

or

The grace of our Lord Jesus Christ, and the love of God, and the fellowship of the Holy Ghost, be with us all evermore. **Amen.

Funeral Rite
The Roman Catholic Church

I RITE OF COMMITTAL AT A CREMATORIUM

This order of service is used when cremation immediately follows a funeral liturgy in church.

INTRODUCTORY RITES

After a brief invitation by the minister a hymn or song may be sung. A scripture verse and a prayer follow.

SIGNS OF FAREWELL

The coffin may now be sprinkled with holy water and incensed, or this may take place at the end of the rite.
The family and other mourners may also sprinkle the coffin with holy water now or at the end of the rite if the coffin remains in view.

COMMITTAL

The minister then says the words of committal during or after which the coffin may be removed from view.

INTERCESSIONS

After each intention the reader says one of the following:

> Lord, in your mercy.

All   **Hear our prayer.**

> We pray to the Lord.

All   **Lord, hear our prayer.**

At the funeral of a child:

> To you we pray.

All   **Bless us and keep us, O Lord.**

51

THE LORD'S PRAYER

All say the Lord's Prayer together after the minister's introduction.

**Our Father, who art in heaven,
hallowed be thy name.
Thy kingdom come.
Thy will be done on earth, as it is in heaven.
Give us this day our daily bread,
and forgive us our trespasses,
as we forgive those who trespass against us,
and lead us not into temptation
but deliver us from evil.**

A concluding prayer follows.

CONCLUDING RITE

PRAYER OVER THE PEOPLE

The minister says:

Bow your heads and pray for God's blessing.

All pray silently. The minister, with hands outstretched over the people, then says a prayer which concludes.

We ask this through Christ our Lord.

All   Amen.

The minister then says the following:

Eternal rest grant unto him/her, O Lord.

All   And let perpetual light shine upon him/her.

May he/she rest in peace.

All   Amen.

May his/her soul and the souls of all the faithful departed, through the mercy of God, rest in peace.

All   Amen.

BLESSING

A   A minister who is a priest or deacon says:

May the peace of God,
which is beyond all understanding,
keep your hearts and minds
in the knowledge and love of God
and of his Son, our Lord Jesus Christ.

All   Amen.

May almighty God bless you,
the Father, and the Son, and the Holy Spirit.

All   Amen.

B   A minister who is a priest or deacon says:

May the love of God and the peace of the Lord Jesus Christ console
you
and gently wipe every tear from your eyes.

All   Amen.

May almighty God bless you,
the Father, and the Son, and the Holy Spirit.

All   Amen.

C   A lay minister invokes God's blessing and signs himself or
     herself with the sign of the cross, saying:

May the love of God and the peace of the Lord Jesus Christ
bless and console us
and gently wipe every tear from our eyes:
in the name of the Father,
and of the Son, and of the Holy Spirit.

All   Amen.

DISMISSAL

The minister then concludes:

Go in the peace of Christ.

All   Thanks be to God.

A hymn of song may conclude the rite. Some sign or gesture of
leave-taking may be made.

II RITE OF COMMITTAL AT A CREMATORIUM WITH FINAL COMMENDATION

This order of service is used when the funeral liturgy has taken place elsewhere or at another time.

GREETING

The minister welcomes the funeral party. The response to the greeting is:

All   **And also with you.**

After a brief invitation by the minister a hymn or song may be sung. A scripture verse follows.

The minister then invites the assembly to pray, after which there is a short period of silence.

The coffin may now be sprinkled with holy water and incensed or this may take place during or after the Song of Farewell.

At this point the mourners may be invited to sprinkle the coffin or it may be done at the end of the rite if the coffin remains in view.

SONG OF FAREWELL

The Song of Farewell is then sung.

One of the following texts or another suitable hymn or song may be sung.

A   I know that my Redeemer lives,
      And on that final day of days,
      His voice shall bid me rise again:
      Unending joy, unceasing praise!
      This hope I cherish in my heart:
      To stand on earth, my flesh restored,
      And, not a stranger but a friend,
      Behold my Saviour and my Lord.
              Tune: LM, for example, Duke Street

B   Saints of God, come to his/her aid!
      Hasten to meet him/her, angels of the Lord!

All   **Receive his/her soul and present him/her**
            to God the Most High.

May Christ, who called you, take you to himself;
may angels lead you to the bosom of Abraham.

All   **Receive his/her soul and present him/her
to God the Most High.**

Eternal rest grant unto him/her, O Lord,
and let perpetual light shine upon him/her.

All   **Receive his/her soul and present him/her
to God the Most High.**

PRAYER OF COMMENDATION AND COMMITTAL

The minister then says a prayer during or after which the coffin may
be removed from view.

CONCLUDING RITE

PRAYER OVER THE PEOPLE

The minister says:

Bow your heads and pray for God's blessing.

All pray silently. The minister, with hands outstretched over the
people, says a prayer which concludes.

We ask this through Christ our Lord.

All   **Amen.**

The minister then says the following:

Eternal rest grant unto him/her, O Lord.

All   **And let perpetual light shine upon him/her.**

May he/she rest in peace.

All   **Amen.**

May his/her soul and the souls of all the faithful departed, through
the mercy of God, rest in peace.

All   **Amen.**

BLESSING

A   A minister who is a priest or deacon says:

May the peace of God,
which is beyond all understanding,
keep your hearts and minds
in the knowledge and love of God
and of his Son, our Lord Jesus Christ.

All   Amen.

May almighty God bless you,
the Father, and the Son, and the Holy Spirit.

All   Amen.

B   A minister who is a priest or deacon says:

May the love of God and the peace of the Lord Jesus Christ console
you
and gently wipe every tear from your eyes.

All   Amen.

May almighty God bless you,
the Father, and the Son, and the Holy Spirit.

All   Amen.

C   A lay minister invokes God's blessing and signs himself or
     herself with the sign of the cross, saying:

May the love of God and the peace of the Lord Jesus Christ
bless and console us
and gently wipe every tear from our eyes:
in the name of the Father,
and of the Son, and of the Holy Spirit.

All   Amen.

DISMISSAL

The minister then concludes:

Go in the peace of Christ.

All   Thanks be to God.

A hymn or song may conclude the rite. Some sign or gesture of
leave-taking may be made.

III RITE OF COMMITTAL FOR CREMATION

This order of service is used when only one funeral liturgy takes place, at the time of committal itself.

INTRODUCTORY RITES
GREETING

At or near the entrance to the chapel, the minister welcomes the funeral party. The response to the greeting is:

All   **And also with you.**

SPRINKLING WITH HOLY WATER

The minister may sprinkle the coffin with holy water as a reminder that those who have died shared in Christ's life by their baptism.

ENTRANCE PROCESSION

During the procession into the chapel a psalm, a hymn or a song may be sung. After the procession a white pall, a symbol of the baptismal garment, and other Christian symbols (eg. a bible or a cross) may be placed on the coffin.

INVITATION TO PRAYER

All remain standing. The minister invites those present to pray.

OPENING PRAYER

After a brief period of silence the minister leads the assembly in prayer.

LITURGY OF THE WORD
SCRIPTURE READING

All sit. A reader proclaims a text from the Old or New Testament and concludes with:

> This is the Word of the Lord.

All   **Thanks be to God.**

A psalm is now sung or said. This may be followed by a reading from the New Testament.

All stand to greet the Gospel. Before a deacon or priest proclaims the Gospel he says:

> The Lord be with you.

All   **And also with you.**

A reading from the holy Gospel according to . . .

All   **Glory to you, Lord.**

At the end of the Gospel he says:

> This is the Gospel of the Lord.

All   **Praise to you, Lord Jesus Christ.**

All sit. A homily based on the readings is given to help those present find strength and hope in God's saving word.

GENERAL INTERCESSIONS

All stand. After each intention the reader says one of the following:

> Lord, in your mercy.

All   **Hear our prayer.**

> We pray to the Lord.

All   **Lord, hear our prayer.**

At the funeral of a child:

> To you we pray.

All   **Bless us and keep us, O Lord.**

58

THE LORD'S PRAYER

All say the Lord's Prayer together after the minister's introduction.

Our Father, who art in heaven,
hallowed be thy name.
Thy kingdom come.
Thy will be done on earth, as it is in heaven.
Give us this day our daily bread,
and forgive us our trespasses,
as we forgive those who trespass against us,
and lead us not into temptation
but deliver us from evil.

A concluding prayer follows.

FINAL COMMENDATION

A member or a friend of the family may now speak in remembrance of the deceased.
The minister invites the assembly to pray, after which there is a short period of silence.
The coffin may now be sprinkled with holy water and incensed or this may take place during or after the Song of Farewell.
At this point the mourners may be invited to sprinkle the coffin, or it may be done at the end of the rite if the coffin remains in view.

SONG OF FAREWELL

The Song of Farewell is then sung.
One of the following texts or another suitable hymn or song may be sung.

A   I know that my Redeemer lives,
          And on that final day of days,
          His voice shall bid me rise again:
          Unending joy, unceasing praise!

          This hope I cherish in my heart:
          To stand on earth, my flesh restored,
          And, not a stranger but a friend,
          Behold my Saviour and my Lord.
               Tune: LM, for example, Duke Street.

B   Saints of God, come to his/her aid!
            Hasten to meet him/her, angels of the Lord!

All   **Receive his/her soul and present him/her
to God the Most High.**

May Christ, who called you, take you to himself;
may angels lead you to the bosom of Abraham.

All   **Receive his/her soul and present him/her
to God the Most High.**

Eternal rest grant unto him/her, O Lord,
and let perpetual light shine upon him/her.

All   **Receive his/her soul and present him/her
to God the Most High.**

PRAYER OF COMMENDATION AND COMMITTAL

The minister then says a prayer during or after which the coffin may be removed from view.

CONCLUDING RITE

PRAYER OVER THE PEOPLE

The minister says:

Bow your heads and pray for God's blessing.

All pray silently. The minister, with hands outstretched over the people, says a prayer which concludes:

We ask this through Christ our Lord.

All   **Amen.**

The minister then says the following:

Eternal rest grant unto him/her, O Lord.

All   **And let perpetual light shine upon him/her.**

May he/she rest in peace.

All   **Amen.**

May his/her soul and the souls of all the faithful departed, through the mercy of God, rest in peace.

All   **Amen.**

BLESSING

A A minister who is a priest or deacon says:

May the peace of God,
which is beyond all understanding,
keep your hearts and minds
in the knowledge and love of God
and of his Son, our Lord Jesus Christ.

All Amen.

May almighty God bless you,
the Father, and the Son, and the Holy Spirit.

All Amen.

B A minister who is a priest or deacon says:

May the love of God and the peace of the Lord Jesus Christ console you
and gently wipe every tear from your eyes.

All Amen.

May almighty God bless you,
the Father, and the Son, and the Holy Spirit.

All Amen.

C A lay minister invokes God's blessing and signs himself or
herself with the sign of the cross, saying:

May the love of God and the peace of the Lord Jesus Christ
bless and console us
and gently wipe every tear from our eyes:
in the name of the Father,
and of the Son, and of the Holy Spirit.

All Amen.

DISMISSAL

The minister then concludes:

Go in the peace of Christ.

All Thanks be to God.

A hymn or song may conclude the rite. Some sign or gesture of
leave-taking may be made.

61

IV RITE OF COMMITTAL FOR BURIAL

This order of service is used when only one funeral liturgy takes place, at the time of committal itself.

INTRODUCTORY RITES

GREETING

At or near the entrance to the chapel, the minister welcomes the funeral party. The response to the greeting is:

All   And also with you.

SPRINKLING WITH HOLY WATER

The minister may sprinkle the coffin with holy water as a reminder that those who have died shared in Christ's life by their baptism.

ENTRANCE PROCESSION

During the procession into the chapel a psalm, a hymn or a song may be sung.

After the procession a white pall, a symbol of the baptismal garment, and other Christian symbols (eg. a bible or a cross) may be placed on the coffin.

INVITATION TO PRAYER

All remain standing. The minister invites those present to pray.

OPENING PRAYER

After a brief period of silence the minister leads the assembly in prayer.

LITURGY OF THE WORD

SCRIPTURE READING

All sit. A reader proclaims a text from the Old or New Testament and concludes with:

This is the Word of the Lord.

All   Thanks be to God.

A psalm is now sung or said. This may be followed by a reading from the New Testament.

All stand to greet the Gospel. Before a deacon or priest proclaims the Gospel he says:

>The Lord be with you.

All   **And also with you.**

>A reading from the holy Gospel according to . . .

All   **Glory to you, Lord.**

At the end of the Gospel he says:

>This is the Gospel of the Lord.

All   **Praise to you, Lord Jesus Christ.**

All sit. A homily based on the readings is given to help those present find strength and hope in God's saving word.

GENERAL INTERCESSIONS

All stand. After each intention the reader says one of the following:

>Lord, in your mercy.

All   **Hear our prayer.**

>We pray to the Lord.

All   **Lord, hear our prayer.**

At the funeral of a child:

>To you we pray.

All   **Bless us and keep us, O Lord.**

THE LORD'S PRAYER

All say the Lord's Prayer together after the minister's introduction.

**Our Father, who art in heaven,
hallowed be thy name.
Thy kingdom come.
Thy will be done on earth, as it is in heaven.
Give us this day our daily bread,
and forgive us our trespasses,
as we forgive those who trespass against us,
and lead us not into temptation
but deliver us from evil.**

A concluding prayer follows.

FINAL COMMENDATION

A member or a friend of the family may now speak in remembrance of the deceased.

The minister invites the assembly to pray, after which there is a short period of silence.

The coffin may now be sprinkled with holy water and incensed or this may take place during or after the Song of Farewell.

SONG OF FAREWELL

The Song of Farewell is then sung.

One of the following texts or another suitable hymn or song may be sung.

A   I know that my Redeemer lives,
And on that final day of days,
His voice shall bid me rise again:
Unending joy, unceasing praise!

This hope I cherish in my heart:
To stand on earth, my flesh restored,
And, not a stranger but a friend,
Behold my Saviour and my Lord.
           Tune: LM, for example, Duke Street

B   Saints of God, come to his/her aid!
Hasten to meet him/her, angels of the Lord!

All   **Receive his/her soul and present him/her
to God the Most High.**

May Christ, who called you, take you to himself;
may angels lead you to the bosom of Abraham.

All   **Receive his/her soul and present him/her
to God the Most High.**

Eternal rest grant unto him/her, O Lord,
and let perpetual light shine upon him/her.

All   **Receive his/her soul and present him/her
to God the Most High.**

The minister concludes with a final prayer

PROCESSION TO THE PLACE OF COMMITTAL

The minister then says:

In peace let us take N. to his/her place of rest.

During the procession one or more of the following texts may be sung:

A   The following antiphon may be sung with verses from Psalm 24(25).

May the angels lead you into paradise;
may the martyrs come to welcome you
and take you to the holy city,
the new and eternal Jerusalem.

B   The following antiphon may be sung with verses from Psalm 114(116), or separately

May choirs of angels welcome you
and lead you to the bosom of Abraham;
and where Lazarus is poor no longer
may you find eternal rest.

C   May saints and angels lead you on,
Escorting you where Christ has gone.
Now he has called you, come to him
Who sits above the seraphim.

Come to the peace of Abraham
And to the supper of the Lamb:
Come to the glory of the blessed,
And to perpetual light and rest.

D   Another suitable psalm may also be used.

The committal at the graveside now follows.

A Selection
of Hymns

1 Abide with me; fast falls the eventide:
   The darkness deepens; Lord, with me abide:
   When other helpers fail, and comforts flee,
   Help of the helpless, O abide with me.

2 Swift to its close ebbs out life's little day;
   Earth's joys grow dim, its glories pass away;
   Change and decay in all around I see:
   O thou who changest not, abide with me.

3 I need thy presence every passing hour;
   What but thy grace can foil the tempter's power?
   Who like thyself my guide and stay can be?
   Through cloud and sunshine, Lord, abide with me.

4 I fear no foe with thee at hand to bless;
   Ills have no weight, and tears no bitterness.
   Where is death's sting? Where, grave, thy victory?
   I triumph still, if thou abide with me.

5 Hold thou thy cross before my closing eyes;
   Shine through the gloom, and point me to the skies:
   Heaven's morning breaks, and earth's vain shadows flee;
   In life, in death, O Lord, abide with me.

1 Alleluia! sing to Jesus!
   His the sceptre, his the throne;
   Alleluia! his the triumph,
   His the victory alone:
   Hark! the songs of peaceful Sion
   Thunder like a mighty flood;
   Jesus out of every nation
   Hath redeemed us by his blood.

2 Alleluia! not as orphans
   Are we left in sorrow now;
   Alleluia! he is near us,
   Faith believes, nor questions how:
   Though the cloud from sight received him,
   When the forty days were o'er,
   Shall our hearts forget his promise,
   'I am with you evermore'?

3 Alleluia! Bread of angels,
   Thou on earth our food, our stay;
   Alleluia! here the sinful
   Flee to thee from day to day:
   Intercessor, friend of sinners,
   Earth's redeemer, plead for me,
   Where the songs of all the sinless
   Sweep across the crystal sea.

1 Amazing grace! How sweet the sound
  That saved a wretch like me.
  I once was lost but now I'm found,
  Was blind, but now I see.

2 'Twas grace that taught my heart to fear,
  And grace my fears relieved.
  How precious did that grace appear
  The hour I first believed.

3 Through many dangers, toils and snares
  I have already come.
  'Tis grace hath brought me safe thus far,
  And grace will lead me home.

4 The Lord has promised good to me;
  His word my hope secures.
  He will my shield and portion be
  As long as life endures.

5 "Yes when this heart and flesh shall fail,
  And mortal life shall cease,
  I shall possess within the vale
  A life of joy and peace.

6 When we've been there ten thousand years,
  Bright shining as the sun,
  We've no less days to sing God's praise,
  Than when we first begun."

1 Blest are the pure in heart,
   For they shall see our God,
   The secret of the Lord is theirs,
   Their soul is Christ's abode.

2 The Lord, who left the heavens
   Our life and peace to bring,
   To dwell in lowliness with men,
   Their pattern and their King;

3 Still to the lowly soul
   He doth himself impart,
   And for his dwelling and his throne
   Chooseth the pure in heart

4 Lord, we thy presence seek;
   May ours this blessing be;
   Give us a pure and lowly heart,
   A temple meet for thee.

1 Dear Lord and Father of mankind,
  Forgive our foolish ways!
  Re-clothe us in our rightful mind,
  In purer lives thy service find,
  In deeper reverence praise.

2 In simple trust like theirs who heard,
  Beside the Syrian sea,
  The gracious calling of the Lord,
  Let us, like them, without a word
  Rise up and follow thee.

3 O Sabbath rest by Galilee!
  O calm of hills above,
  Where Jesus knelt to share with thee
  The silence of eternity,
  Interpreted by love!

4 Drop thy still dews of quietness,
  Till all our strivings cease;
  Take from our souls the strain and stress,
  And let our ordered lives confess
  The beauty of thy peace.

5 Breathe through the heats of our desire
  Thy coolness and thy balm;
  Let sense be dumb, let flesh retire;
  Speak through the earthquake, wind, and fire,
  O still small voice of calm!

1 Eternal Father, strong to save,
   Whose arm doth bind the restless wave,
   Who bidd'st the mighty ocean deep
   Its own appointed limits keep;
   O hear us when we cry to thee
   For those in peril on the sea.

2 O Saviour, whose almighty word
   The winds and waves submissive heard,
   Who walkedst on the foaming deep,
   And calm amid its rage didst sleep:
   O hear us when we cry to thee
   For those in peril on the sea.

3 O sacred Spirit, who didst brood
   Upon the chaos dark and rude,
   Who bad'st its angry tumult cease,
   And gavest light and life and peace:
   O hear us when we cry to thee
   For those in peril on the sea.

4 O trinity of love and power,
   Our brethren shield in danger's hour;
   From rock and tempest, fire and foe,
   Protect them whereso'er they go:
   And ever let there rise to thee
   Glad hymns of praise from land and sea.

1 For all the saints who from their labours rest,
  Who thee by faith before the world confessed,
  Thy name, O Jesu, be for ever blest.
                    Alleluia!

2 Thou wast their rock, their fortress and their might;
  Thou, Lord, their captain in the well-fought fight;
  Thou, in the darkness, still their one true Light.
                    Alleluia!

3 O blest communion, fellowship divine!
  We feebly struggle, they in glory shine;
  Yet all are one in thee, for all are thine.
                    Alleluia!

4 And when the strife is fierce, the warfare long,
  Steals on the ear the distant triumph song,
  And hearts are brave again and arms are strong.
                    Alleluia!

5 But lo, there breaks a yet more glorious day;
  The saints triumphant rise in bright array:
  The King of Glory passes on his way.
                    Alleluia!

6 From earth's wide bounds, from ocean's farthest coast,
  Through gates of pearl streams in the countless host,
  Singing to Father, Son, and Holy Ghost.
                    Alleluia!

1 Great is thy faithfulness, O God my Father,
   There is no shadow of turning with thee;
   Thou changest not, thy compassions they fail not,
   As thou hast been thou for ever wilt be.

   Great is thy faithfulness,
   Great is thy faithfulness;
   Morning by morning
   New mercies I see;
   All I have needed
   Thy hand hath provided,—
   great is thy faithfulness,
   Lord unto me!

2 Summer and winter, and spring-time and harvest,
   Sun, moon and stars in their courses above,
   Join with all nature in manifold witness
   To thy great faithfulness,
   Mercy and love.

   Great is thy faithfulness ...

3 Pardon for sin, and a peace that endureth,
   Thine own dear presence to cheer and to guide;
   Strength for today and bright hope for tomorrow,
   Blessings all mine, with ten thousand beside!

   Great is thy faithfulness ...

1 Guide me, O thou great Redeemer,
  Pilgrim through this barren land;
  I am weak, but thou art mighty;
  Hold me with thy powerful hand:
  Bread of heaven,
  Feed me now and evermore.

2 Open now the crystal fountain,
  Whence the healing stream doth flow;
  Let the fiery cloudy pillar
  Lead me all my journey through:
  Strong deliverer,
  Be thou still my strength and shield.

3 When I tread the verge of Jordan,
  Bid my anxious fears subside;
  Death of death, and hell's destruction,
  Land me safe on Canaan's side:
  Songs and praises
  I will ever give to thee.

1 How sweet the name of Jesus sounds
  In a believer's ear!
  It soothes our sorrows, heals our wounds,
  And drives away our fear.

2 It makes the wounded spirit whole,
  And calms the troubled breast;
  'Tis manna to the hungry soul,
  And to the weary rest.

3 Dear name! the rock on which I build,
  My shield and hiding-place,
  My never-failing treasury filled
  With boundless stores of grace.

4 Jesus! my shepherd, brother, friend,
  My prophet, priest, and king,
  My Lord, my life, my way, my end,
  Accept the praise I bring.

5 Weak is the effort of my heart,
  And cold my warmest thought;
  But when I see thee as thou art,
  I'll praise thee as I ought.

6 Till then I would thy love proclaim
  With every fleeting breath;
  And may the music of thy name
  Refresh my soul in death.

1 I am the Bread of Life;
   He who comes to Me shall not hunger;
   He who believes in Me shall not thirst.
   No one can come to Me unless the
   Father draw him.
   And I will raise him up,
   And I will raise him up,
   And I will raise him up,
   On the last day.

2 The bread that I will give
   Is My flesh for the life of the world;
   And he who eats of this bread,
   He shall live for ever
   He shall live for ever.
   And I will raise ...

3 Unless you eat
   Of the flesh of the Son of Man
   And drink of His blood,
   And drink of His blood,
   You shall not have life within you.
   And I will raise ...

4 I am the Resurrection,
   I am the Life;
   He who believes in Me,
   Even if he die, he shall live for ever.
   And I will raise ...

5 Yes, Lord, we believe
   That You are the Christ,
   The Son of God,
   Who has come into the world.
   And I will raise ...

1 Immortal, invisible, God only wise,
   In light inaccessible hid from our eyes,
   Most blessèd, most glorious, the Ancient of Days,
   Almighty, victorious, thy great name we praise.

2 Unresting, unhasting, and silent as light,
   Nor wanting, nor wasting, thou rulest in might;
   Thy justice like mountains high soaring above
   Thy clouds which are fountains of goodness and love.

3 To all life thou givest—to both great and small;
   In all life thou livest, the true life of all;
   We blossom and flourish as leaves on the tree,
   And wither and perish—but nought changeth thee.

4 Great Father of glory, pure Father of light,
   Thine angels adore thee, all veiling their sight;
   All laud we would render: O help us to see
   'Tis only the splendour of light hideth thee.

1 In heavenly love abiding,
  No change my heart shall fear;
  And safe is such confiding,
  For nothing changes here.
  The storm may roar around me,
  My heart may low be laid;
  But God is round about me:
  How can I be dismayed?

2 Wherever he may guide me,
  No want shall turn me back;
  My shepherd is beside me,
  And nothing can I lack;
  His wisdom ever waketh,
  His sight is never dim;
  He knows the way he taketh,
  And I will walk with him.

3 Green pastures are before me,
  Which yet I have not seen;
  Bright skies will soon be o'er me,
  Where dark the clouds have been.
  My hope I cannot measure,
  My path to life is free;
  My Saviour hath my treasure,
  And he will walk with me.

1 Jesus lives! thy terrors now
  Can no more, O death, appal us;
  Jesus lives! by this we know
  Thou, O grave, canst not enthral us.
                              Alleluia!

2 Jesus lives! henceforth is death
  But the gate of life immortal:
  This shall calm our trembling breath,
  When we pass its gloomy portal.
                              Alleluia!

3 Jesus lives! for us he died;
  Then, alone to Jesus living,
  Pure in heart may we abide,
  Glory to our Saviour giving.
                              Alleluia!

4 Jesus lives! our hearts know well
  Naught from us his love shall sever;
  Life nor death nor powers of hell
  Tear us from his keeping ever.
                              Alleluia!

5 Jesus lives! to him the throne
  Over all the world is given:
  May we go where he is gone,
  Rest and reign with him in heaven.
                              Alleluia!

1 Jesus, lover of my soul,
  Let me to thy bosom fly,
  While the nearer waters roll,
  While the tempest still is high:
  Hide me, O my Saviour, hide,
  Till the storm of life be past:
  Safe into the haven guide,
  O receive my soul at last.

2 Other refuge have I none,
  Hangs my helpless soul on thee;
  Leave, ah! leave me not alone,
  Still support and comfort me:
  All my trust on thee is stayed:
  All my help from thee I bring:
  Cover my defenceless head
  With the shadow of thy wing.

3 Thou, O Christ, art all I want;
  More than all in thee I find;
  Raise the fallen, cheer the faint,
  Heal the sick and lead the blind.
  Just and holy is thy name;
  I am all unrighteousness:
  False and full of sin I am;
  Thou art full of truth and grace.

4 Plenteous grace with thee is found,
  Grace to cover all my sin;
  Let the healing streams abound,
  Make and keep me pure within:
  Thou of life the fountain art,
  Freely let me take of thee:
  Spring thou up within my heart,
  Rise to all eternity.

81

1 Just as I am, without one plea
But that thy blood was shed for me,
And that thou bidd'st me come to thee,
O Lamb of God, I come.

2 Just as I am, though tossed about
With many a conflict, many a doubt,
Fightings within, and fears without,
O Lamb of God, I come.

3 Just as I am, poor, wretched, blind;
Sight, riches, healing of the mind,
Yea all I need, in thee to find,
O Lamb of God, I come.

4 Just as I am, thou wilt receive,
Wilt welcome, pardon, cleanse, relieve:
Because thy promise I believe,
O Lamb of God, I come.

5 Just as I am (thy love unknown
Has broken every barrier down),
Now to be thine, yea thine alone,
O Lamb of God, I come.

6 Just as I am, of that free love
The breadth, length, depth and height to prove,
Here for a season then above,
O Lamb of God, I come.

1 Lead us, heavenly Father, lead us
  O'er the world's tempestuous sea;
  Guard us, guide us, keep us, feed us,
  For we have no help but thee;
  Yet possessing every blessing,
  If our God our Father be.

2 Saviour, breathe forgiveness o'er us:
  All our weakness thou dost know;
  Thou didst tread this earth before us,
  Thou didst feel its keenest woe;
  Lone and dreary, faint and weary,
  Through the desert thou didst go.

3 Spirit of our God, descending,
  Fill our hearts with heavenly joy,
  Love with every passion blending,
  Pleasure that can never cloy:
  Thus provided, pardoned, guided,
  Nothing can our peace destroy.

1 Lord of all hopefulness, Lord of all joy,
  Whose trust, ever childlike,
              no cares could destroy:
  Be there at our waking, and give us, we pray,
  Your bliss in our hearts, Lord,
              at the break of the day.

2 Lord of all eagerness, Lord of all faith,
  Whose strong hands were skilled
              at the plane and the lathe:
  Be there at our labours, and give us, we pray,
  Your strength in our hearts, Lord,
              at the noon of the day.

3 Lord of all kindliness, Lord of all grace,
  Your hands swift to welcome,
              your arms to embrace:
  Be there at our homing and give us, we pray,
  Your love in our hearts, Lord,
              at the eve of the day.

4 Lord of all gentleness, Lord of all calm,
  Whose voice is contentment,
              whose presence is balm:
  Be there at our sleeping, and give us, we pray,
  Your peace in our hearts, Lord,
              at the end of the day!

1 Love divine, all loves excelling,
  Joy of heaven, to earth come down,
  Fix in us thy humble dwelling,
  All thy faithful mercies crown.
  Jesus, thou art all compassion,
  Pure unbounded love thou art;
  Visit us with thy salvation,
  Enter every trembling heart.

2 Come, almighty to deliver,
  Let us all thy grace receive;
  Suddenly return, and never,
  Never more thy temples leave.
  Thee we would be always blessing,
  Serve thee as thy hosts above;
  Pray, and praise thee, without ceasing,
  Glory in thy perfect love.

3 Finish then thy new creation:
  Pure and spotless let us be;
  Let us see thy great salvation,
  Perfectly restored in thee;
  Changed from glory into glory,
  Till in heaven we take our place,
  Till we cast our crowns before thee,
  Lost in wonder, love, and praise.

1 Love's redeeming work is done;
  Fought the fight, the battle won:
  Vain the stone, the watch, the seal!
  Christ has burst the gates of hell.

2 Lives again our glorious King;
  Where, O death, is now thy sting?
  Once he died our souls to save;
  Where thy victory, O grave?

3 Soar we now where Christ has led,
  Following our exalted Head;
  Made like him, like him we rise;
  Ours the cross, the grave, the skies.

4 Hail the Lord of earth and heaven!
  Praise to thee by both be given:
  Thee we greet triumphant now;
  Hail, the Resurrection thou!

Sometimes Alleluia is sung between each line

1 Make me a channel of your peace.
Where there is hatred, let me bring your love;
Where there is injury, your pardon, Lord;
And when there's doubt, true faith in you:

O Master, grant that I may never seek
So much to be consoled as to console;
To be understood as to understand;
To be loved as to love with all my soul.

2 Make me a channel of your peace.
Where there's despair in life, let me bring hope;
Where there is darkness, only light;
And where there's sadness, ever joy:

O Master, grant ...

3 Make me a channel of your peace.
It is in pardoning that we are pardoned,
In giving to all men that we receive,
And in dying that we're brought to eternal life.

1 Now thank we all our God,
   With heart and hands and voices,
   Who wondrous things hath done,
   In whom his world rejoices;
   Who from our mother's arms
   Hath blessed us on our way
   With countless gifts of love,
   And still is ours to-day.

2 O may this bounteous God
   Through all our life be near us,
   With ever joyful hearts
   And blessed peace to cheer us;
   And keep us in his grace,
   And guide us when perplexed,
   And free us from all ills
   In this world and the next.

3 All praise and thanks to God
   The Father now be given,
   The Son, and him who reigns
   With them in highest heaven,
   The one eternal God,
   Whom earth and heaven adore,
   For thus it was, is now,
   And shall be evermore.

1 O God, our help in ages past,
   Our hope for years to come,
   Our shelter from the stormy blast,
   And our eternal home;

2 Beneath the shadow of thy throne
   Thy saints have dwelt secure;
   Sufficient is thine arm alone,
   And our defence is sure.

3 Before the hills in order stood,
   Or earth received her frame,
   From everlasting thou art God,
   To endless years the same.

4 A thousand ages in thy sight
   Are like an evening gone;
   Short as the watch that ends the night
   Before the rising sun.

5 O God, our help in ages past,
   Our hope for years to come,
   Be thou our guard while troubles last,
   And our eternal home.

1 O Lord my God! When I in awesome wonder
  Consider all the works thy hands have made:
  I see the stars, I hear the mighty thunder,
  Thy pow'r throughout the universe displayed:

  Then sings my soul, my Saviour God to thee
  How great thou art! How great thou art!
  Then sings my soul, my Saviour God to thee
  How great thou art! How great thou art!

2 And when I think that God his Son not sparing,
  Sent him to die, I scarce can take it in;
  That on the cross, my burden gladly bearing,
  He bled and died to take away my sin:

  Then sings my soul, my Saviour God to thee
  How great thou art! How great thou art!
  Then sings my soul, my Saviour God to thee
  How great thou art! How great thou art!

3 When Christ shall come with shout of acclamation
  To take me home, what joy shall fill my heart!
  Then shall I bow in humble adoration,
  And there proclaim, My God how great thou art.

  Then sings my soul, my Saviour God to thee
  How great thou art! How great thou art!
  Then sings my soul, my Saviour God to thee
  How great thou art! How great thou art!

1 O love that wilt not let me go,
   I rest my weary soul in thee:
   I give thee back the life I owe,
   That in thine ocean depths its flow
   May richer, fuller, be.

2 O light that followest all my way,
   I yield my flickering torch to thee:
   My heart restores its borrowed ray,
   That in thy sunshine's blaze its day
   May brighter, fairer be.

3 O joy that seekest me through pain,
   I cannot close my heart to thee:
   I trace the rainbow through the rain,
   And feel the promise is not vain
   That morn shall tearless be.

4 O cross that liftest up my head,
   I dare not ask to fly from thee:
   I lay in dust life's glory dead,
   And from the ground there blossoms red
   Life that shall endless be.

1 On a hill far away stood an old rugged cross,
  The emblem of suff'ring and shame;
  And I loved that old cross where the dearest and best
  For a world of lost sinners was slain.

  So I'll cherish the old rugged cross,
  Till my trophies at last I lay down;
  I will cling to the old rugged cross
  And exchange it someday for a crown.

2 Oh that old rugged cross, so despised by the world,
  Has a wondrous attraction for me:
  For the dear Lamb of God left his glory above
  To bear it to dark Calvary.

  So I'll cherish the old rugged cross,

3 In the old rugged cross, stained with blood so divine,
  A wondrous beauty I see.
  For 'twas on that old cross Jesus suffered and died
  To pardon and sanctify me.

  So I'll cherish the old rugged cross,

4 To the old rugged cross I will ever be true,
  Its shame and reproach gladly bear.
  Then he'll call me some day to my home far away,
  There his glory for ever I'll share.

  So I'll cherish the old rugged cross,

1 Peace, perfect peace, in this dark world of sin?
  The blood of Jesus whispers peace within.

2 Peace, perfect peace, by thronging duties pressed?
  To do the will of Jesus, this is rest.

3 Peace, perfect peace, with sorrows surging round?
  On Jesus' bosom naught but calm is found.

4 Peace, perfect peace, with loved ones far away?
  In Jesus' keeping we are safe and they.

5 Peace, perfect peace, our future all unknown?
  Jesus we know, and he is on the throne.

6 Peace, perfect peace, death shadowing us and ours?
  Jesus has vanquished death and all its powers.

7 It is enough: earth's struggles soon shall cease,
  And Jesus call us to heaven's perfect peace.

1 Praise, my soul, the King of heaven;
   To his feet thy tribute bring.
   Ransomed, healed, restored, forgiven,
   Who like me his praise should sing?
   Praise him! Praise Him!
   Praise the everlasting King.

2 Praise him for his grace and favour
   To our forbears in distress;
   Praise him still the same for ever,
   Slow to chide, and swift to bless.
   Praise him! Praise him!
   Glorious in his faithfulness.

3 Father-like, he tends and spares us;
   Well our feeble frame he knows;
   In his hands he gently bears us,
   Rescues us from all our foes.
   Praise him! Praise him!
   Widely as his mercy flows.

4 Angels, help us to adore him;
   Ye behold him face to face;
   Sun and moon, bow down before him;
   Dwellers all in time and space.
   Praise him! Praise him!
   Praise with us the God of grace.

1 Rock of ages, cleft for me,
 Let me hide myself in thee;
 Let the water and the blood,
 From thy riven side which flowed,
 Be of sin the double cure:
 Cleanse me from its guilt and power.

2 Not the labours of my hands
 Can fulfil thy law's demands;
 Could my zeal no respite know,
 Could my tears for ever flow,
 All for sin could not atone:
 Thou must save, and thou alone.

3 Nothing in my hand I bring,
 Simply to thy cross I cling,
 Naked, come to thee for dress;
 Helpless, look to thee for grace;
 Foul, I to the fountain fly;
 Wash me, Saviour, or I die.

4 While I draw this fleeting breath,
 When my eyelids close in death,
 When I soar through tracts unknown,
 See thee on thy judgement throne;
 Rock of ages, cleft for me,
 Let me hide myself in thee.

1 The day thou gavest, Lord, is ended,
 The darkness falls at thy behest;
 To thee our morning hymns ascended,
 Thy praise shall sanctify our rest.

2 We thank thee that thy church unsleeping,
 While earth rolls onward into light,
 Through all the world her watch is keeping,
 And rests not now by day or night.

3 As o'er each continent and island
 The dawn leads on another day,
 The voice of prayer is never silent,
 Nor dies the strain of praise away.

4 The sun that bids us rest is waking
 Our friends beneath the western sky,
 And hour by hour fresh lips are making
 Thy wondrous doings heard on high.

5 So be it, Lord; thy throne shall never,
 Like earth's proud empires, pass away;
 Thy kingdom stands, and grows for ever,
 Till all thy creatures own thy sway.

1 The King of love my Shepherd is,
   Whose goodness faileth never;
   I nothing lack if I am his
   And he is mine for ever.

2 Where streams of living water flow
   My ransomed soul he leadeth,
   And where the verdant pastures grow
   With food celestial feedeth.

3 Perverse and foolish oft I strayed,
   But yet in love he sought me,
   And on his shoulder gently laid,
   And home rejoicing brought me.

4 In death's dark vale I fear no ill
   With thee, dear Lord, beside me;
   Thy rod and staff my comfort still,
   Thy cross before to guide me.

5 Thou spread'st a table in my sight;
   Thy unction grace bestoweth;
   And O what transport of delight
   From thy pure chalice floweth!

6 And so through all the length of days
   Thy goodness faileth never:
   Good Shepherd, may I sing thy praise
   Within thy house for ever.

1 The Lord's my Shepherd, I'll not want,
   He makes me down to lie
   In pastures green: he leadeth me
   The quiet waters by.

2 My soul he doth restore again,
   And me to walk doth make
   Within the paths of righteousness,
   E'en for his own name's sake.

3 Yea, though I walk through death's dark vale
   Yet will I fear no ill;
   For thou art with me, and thy rod
   And staff me comfort still.

4 My table thou hast furnished
   In presence of my foes;
   My head thou dost with oil anoint,
   And my cup overflows.

5 Goodness and mercy all my life
   Shall surely follow me;
   And in God's house for evermore
   My dwelling-place shall be.

1 The strife is o'er, the battle done;
   Now is the victor's triumph won;
   O let the song of praise be sung:
                     Alleluia!

2 Death's mightiest powers have done their worst,
   And Jesus hath his foes dispersed;
   Let shouts of praise and joy outburst:
                     Alleluia!

3 On the third morn he rose again
   Glorious in majesty to reign;
   O let us swell the joyful strain:
                     Alleluia!

4 Lord, by the stripes which wounded thee
   From death's dread sting thy servants free,
   That we may live, and sing to thee
                     Alleluia!

1 There is a green hill far away,
  Outside a city wall,
  Where the dear Lord was crucified,
  Who died to save us all.

2 We may not know, we cannot tell,
  What pains he had to bear,
  But we believe it was for us
  He hung and suffered there.

3 He died that we might be forgiven,
  He died to make us good,
  That we might go at last to heaven,
  Saved by his precious blood.

4 There was no other good enough
  To pay the price of sin;
  He only could unlock the gate
  Of heaven, and let us in.

5 O dearly, dearly has he loved,
  And we must love him too,
  And trust in his redeeming blood,
  And try his works to do.

1 There is a Redeemer,
Jesus, God's own Son,
Precious Lamb of God, Messiah,
Holy One.

Thank You, O my Father
For giving us Your Son,
And leaving Your Spirit
Till the work on earth is done.

2 Jesus my Redeemer,
Name above all names,
Precious Lamb of God, Messiah,
O for sinners slain:

Thank You ...

3 When I stand in glory
I will see His face,
And there I'll serve my King for ever
In that holy place.

Thank You ...

1 Thine be the glory, risen, conquering Son,
Endless is the victory thou o'er death hast won;
Angels in bright raiment rolled the stone away,
Kept the folded grave-clothes where thy body lay.

Thine be the glory, risen, conquering Son,
Endless is the victory thou o'er death hast won!

2 Lo! Jesus meets us, risen from the tomb;
Lovingly he greets us, scatters fear and gloom;
Let the church with gladness hymns of triumph sing,
For her Lord now liveth, death hath lost its sting.

Thine be the glory, risen, conquering Son,
Endless is the victory thou o'er death hast won!

3 No more we doubt thee, glorious prince of life;
Life is naught without thee: aid us in our strife;
Make us more than conquerors through thy deathless love;
Bring us safe through Jordan to thy home above.

Thine be the glory, risen, conquering Son,
Endless is the victory thou o'er death hast won!

1 To God be the glory, great things he has done!
So loved he the world that he gave us his Son.
Who yielded his life in atonement for sin,
And opened the life-gate that all may go in.

Praise the Lord! Praise the Lord!
Let the earth hear his voice!
Praise the Lord! Praise the Lord!
Let the people rejoice!
O come to the Father through Jesus his Son;
And give him the glory, great things he has done!

2 O perfect redemption, the purchase of blood,
To every believer the promise of God!
And every offender who truly believes,
That moment from Jesus a pardon receives.

Praise the Lord! Praise the Lord!

3 Great things he has taught us,
Great things he has done,
And great our rejoicing through Jesus the Son;
But purer, and higher, and greater will be
Our wonder, our rapture, when Jesus we see.

Praise the Lord! Praise the Lord!

1 When I survey the wondrous Cross,
  On which the Prince of glory died,
  My richest gain I count but loss,
  And pour contempt on all my pride.

2 Forbid it, Lord, that I should boast
  Save in the death of Christ my God;
  All the vain things that charm me most,
  I sacrifice them to his blood.

3 See from his head, his hands, his feet,
  Sorrow and love flow mingled down;
  Did e'er such love and sorrow meet,
  Or thorns compose so rich a crown?

4 His dying crimson like a robe,
  Spreads o'er his body on the Tree;
  Then am I dead to all the globe,
  And all the globe is dead to me.

5 Were the whole realm of nature mine,
  That were a present far too small;
  Love so amazing, so divine,
  Demands my soul, my life, my all.

Index to Hymns

Sources and Acknowledgements

The Origins of this Book

The Churches' Group (formerly Joint Group) on Funeral Services at Cemeteries and Crematoria, the membership of which is set out on page iv, sponsored in 1985 an ecumenical handbook *Funerals and Ministry to the Bereaved* intended for the use of clergy, funeral directors and crematoria and cemetery staff. During the preparation of this handbook it became clear that a composite Service Book, also sponsored by all the participating Churches, would be welcomed and found pastorally helpful in crematoria and cemetery chapels.

The combined efforts of the Churches' Group, working on this project in consultation with the Free Church Council of Wales and the Joint Liturgical Group, have made it possible to produce two Service Books, this present edition for use in England and a companion edition for use in Wales. Both contain within one volume a set of funeral services which includes at least one service that can be used by each of the five Communions represented on the Churches' Group according to the circumstances of the occasion. The edition for Wales also contains versions of two services and eight hymns in the Welsh language.

Funeral Service prepared by the Joint Liturgical Group

This Service which is © The Joint Liturgical Group is adapted from the Funeral Service in *The Daily Office Revised* published in 1978 and is reproduced with permission.

107

The Joint Liturgical Group was formed in 1963 and includes representatives of the Church of England, the Church of Scotland, the Scottish Episcopal Church, the Baptist Union, the Methodist, Roman Catholic and United Reformed Churches, and the Fellowship of the Churches of Christ, who together develop projects and deal with questions relating to public worship of common concern.

Church of England Services

An Order for the Burial of the Dead and an Order for the Burial of a Child, both from *Alternative Services: First Series*, are © Central Board of Finance of the Church of England and are reproduced by permission.

Funeral Services from *The Alternative Service Book 1980* are © Central Board of Finance of the Church of England and are reproduced by permission. Psalms from the Liturgical Psalter are © English text 1976, 1977, David L. Frost, John A. Emerton, Andrew A. MacIntosh.

The First Series Burial Services are authorised for use in the Provinces of Canterbury and York pursuant to Canon B2 of the Canons of the Church of England until 31st December 1990. The Funeral Services from *The Alternative Service Book 1980* are similarly authorised until 31st December 2000.

Roman Catholic Services

Extracts from the *Order of Christian Funerals* copyright 1989, 1985, International Committee on English in the Liturgy. All rights reserved.

This arrangement copyright 1990, Liturgy Office of the
Catholic Bishops' Conference of England and Wales. All rights
reserved.

Psalm texts from *The Psalms: A New Translation* copyright
The Grail (England) 1963.

Concordat cum Originali Jennifer C. Demolder, Peter M.
Gallacher

Selection of Hymns

The following hymns are copyright and used with permission:

Page No.	Author	Permission granted by
74	T. O. Chisholm	Hope Publishing Co., Carol Stream, Il 60188, USA
77	S. Suzanne Toolan	G. I. A. Publications Inc., Chicago, Il 60638, USA. All rights reserved
84	Jan Struther	Oxford University Press
87	S. Temple	© 1994. Franciscan Communications, Los Angeles CA 90015 USA. All rights reserved
90	S. Hine	Author
101	Melody Green	© 1982, Birdwing Music/ Cherry Lane Music Pub Co, USA. Reproduced by permission of Cherry Lane Music Ltd, London WC2H 0EA. Administered by EMI Music Publishing Ltd.